COLORFUL CHINA

Written by Liang Minling

Translated by Liu Bingwen & Pan Zhongming

Contents

A Colorful World   P004

P007

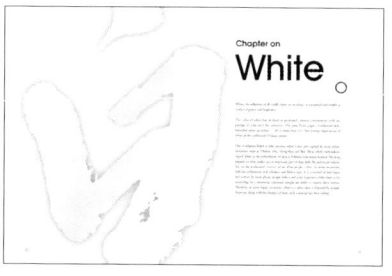
P023

P055

 P069

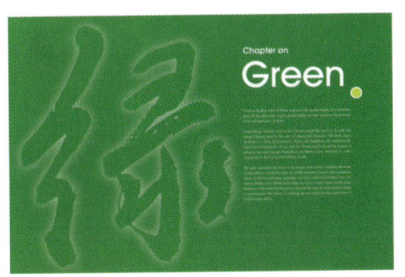 P087

 P105

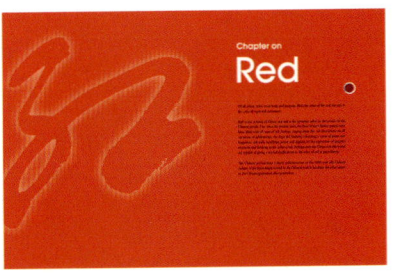 P127

A Colorful World

The world becomes lively because it is decorated with a myriad of colors. In either the countryside of blossoms amid lush green vegetation of nature or cities with metropolis buildings of attractive styles and forms, we are always surrounded by a world of colors.

According to scientists, colors are merely impacts of light of varying waves on the human visual nerves. But to mankind, colors are not just physical phenomena. They are means of emotional expressions, for they convey values, ideas and aspirations. In the long human history, colors have attained profound cultural connotations that transcend their natural attributes.

A sage once said: "Color is a kind of language of the most popular nature among all artistic tools." Color originates in nature, appears in daily life and finds its expression in history. A particular color therefore may become the favorite of one nation, a symbol of a country, the keynote of a culture.

The Chinese are a nation good at using colors. All colors in the great nature may lend tremendous inspirations to the Chinese, whether it is the golden yellow ears of grain crops on the vast Chinese hinterland, the white snow of northern China, the green mountains and rivers of southern China. In the traditional Chinese culture, and its art in particular, colors may present themselves in dazing brilliance of numberless hues or in sober quietness of black, white and varying grays in between; in the majesty of the imperial palaces that hold commoners in awe or in the blue of indigo print garments of rustic folks; in paintings and embroidery of bright tints or in the purity of white porcelain and translucent jade…

And colors have instilled vigor and vitality into the daily life of the Chinese common people. The people of Han nationality in the villages in the Yellow River valley like to paste brightly red scrolls and New-Year pictures on their doors and walls during the Spring Festival. Young ladies of Miao hamlets in the mountainous Southwest China add to the festivity of their national holidays with their national costumes of cloth woven with yarns of black, white, yellow, blue, purple, red and orange colors. On the vast Inner Mongolia grasslands, the herdsmen love to dress in red robes against the backdrop of green grasslands and azure sky with floating puffs of white clouds. At the foot of the snow-capped peaks, Tibetans prefer to have their outer walls plastered in pure white and honor their guests with white silk ceremonial scarves which they call "hata."

Colors in their numerous manifestations are in correspondence to different facets of people's lives. Red, for example, reminds people of festivity and auspice among the Chinese people whereas the color of white sometimes means bad omen in the Han culture. Even colors like bright yellow, deep purple and transparent blue were the monopoly of certain social strata at certain periods of time in Chinese history and those colors with their original attributes lost for long today remain to arouse associations in people's minds.

The richness of colors serves as a deposit of the sentiments and wisdom of the Chinese people and meanwhile it carries the unique cultural memories of the Chinese. It has the function of a key to a special door of the Chinese mind and it is capable of ushering outsiders to savoring the flavors of colorful China.

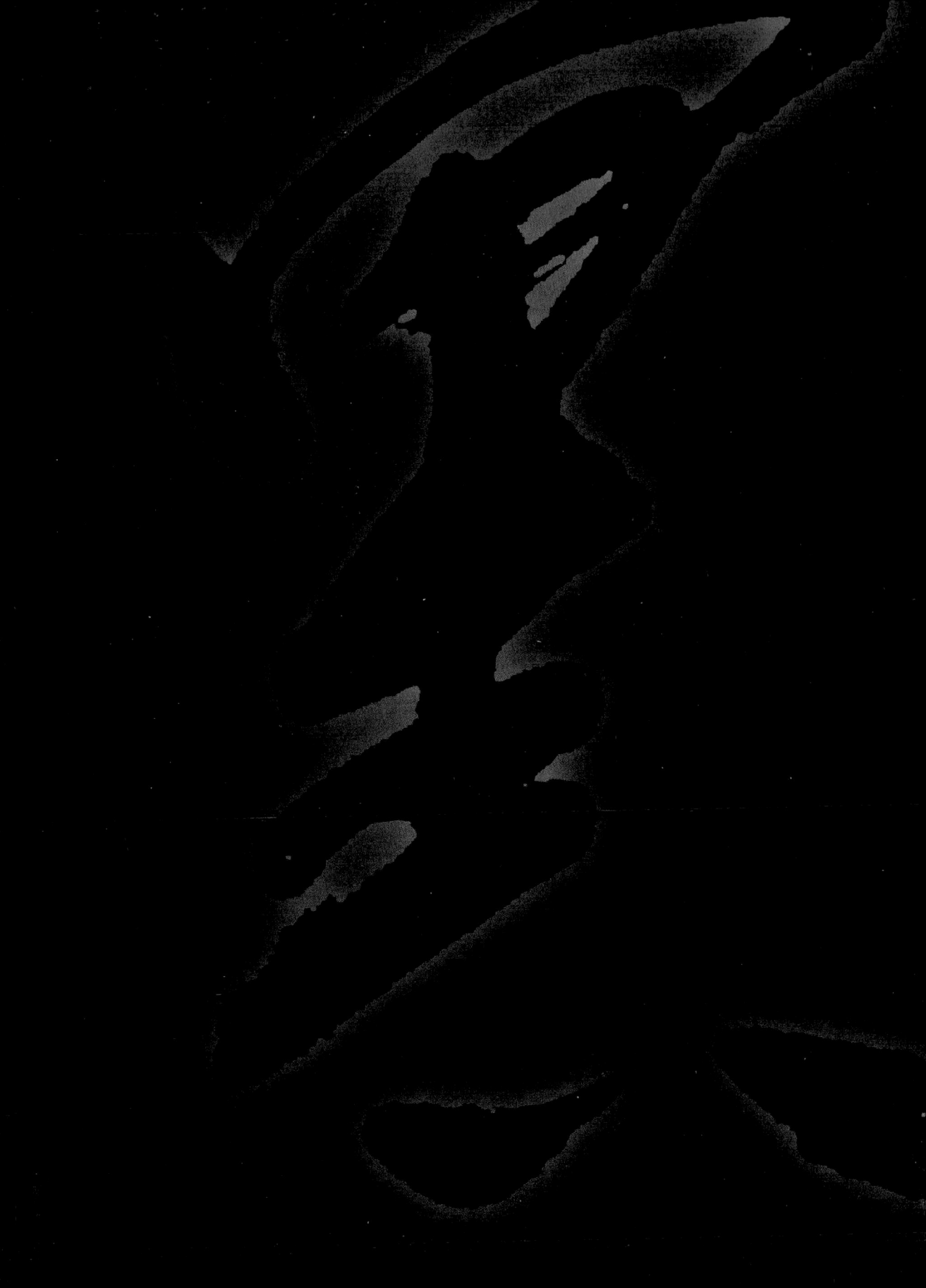

Chapter on Black

Black, the color of night, represents mystery, profundity, gravity and solemnity.

Black is a color of no color, no light. It is seemingly monotonous and dull. Yet, there is no lack of interest in a world of darkness.

The black pottery fired in ancient Chinese kilns is literally jewels of plainness and elegance. The Chinese ink-brush produces flowing black strokes of Chinese calligraphy and traditional paintings that bring out vivid perspectives with varying degrees of black and gray, a proof of the high position of the color of black in traditional Chinese culture. In their pragmatic daily life, the Chinese love gray bricks and black tiles to spell out profound symbols in their time-honored house construction.

In the West, black usually means grief, sorrow or terror. In China, black has different meaning for different nationalities. Han nationality and some other nationalities regard black as an inauspicious and ugly omen. But Yi nationality upholds black. They show respects to black and regard it as beautiful and auspicious. However, in modern life, there are few people who link black with anything inauspicious. On the contrary, black has even become one of the most fashionable colors people are after. Black garment accessories, furniture, sedan cars, computers and mobile phones are a great favor of people.

COLORFUL CHINA

Lijiang River in Guilin, The Guangxi Zhuang Autonomous Region. After night falls, everything is vestured in black.

COLORFUL CHINA

The crescent-shaped black earth belt that stretches in the basins of Songhua River and Liaohe River in Northeast China covers a total area of about 1 million square meters. It is the most fertile and arable land in China. Under the frigid weather in the area, the dead vegetation, after long time decay, finally evolves into a layer of black earth with an average thickness of 30 to 100 cm. Local people often refer its fertility as that "50 grams of black earth can produce 100 grams of edible oil."

This piece of black land is one of the three black earths in the world. (The other two are scattered at the Ukraine plain and the Mississippi River basin in North America.) For many years, the area is the largest grain production base in China, hence the name of "Great Northern Granary".

Wuzhen Town at the northern part of Tongxiang in Zhejiang Province has a history of more than 1,300 years. It is said that because local residents paint a layer of black paint on their walls and black is called "Wu" in the local dialect, the town thus gets the name "Wuzhen".

Upon arriving at Wuzhen, you may discover that this ancient town has really closely connected with black. Looking up, all the roofs are in black. Walking on the narrow and deep streets with stone steps, the wooden walls, doors and windows of the houses along both sides are all in black. On the small river that traverses through the town, small boats with a black cover pass by slowly. The black cover of the boat is a great match to the black tiles on the roof of house on the banks. The water reflects the inverted image of old wooden house on the bank…

The basic color of black has made the town quiet as if time had been halted for several hundred years. The simple and unhurried Wuzhen has a special flavor of the water town in the south of the Yangtze River as if it were a poem and a dream.

COLORFUL CHINA

Archeological finds of ancient pottery shards indicated that ancient Chinese began making pottery some ten thousand years ago, which should be in the early Neolithic Age. By late Neolithic Age some 4,000 years ago, after the decline of red pottery, gray pottery and colored pottery, the art of black pottery sprang up.

Black pottery was characterized by its simplicity in designing and decoration, entirely without decoration or with very little decoration of simple lines or incised holes. The entire body of a black potter is shiningly black. The simplicity of the black pottery articles conveys a profundity through plainness with a powerful artistic impact to the viewer.

With the onset of the Bronze Age, black pottery gradually resigned from the arena of history. However, the art of Chinese black pottery has led people of the succeeding centuries infinitely to marvel at and sing high praise from the bottom of their hearts. People call the art of black pottery "an art of blending earth and fire, integration of strength and beauty".

The black pottery pot unearthed at the Hemudu Culture Relics dating back about 7,000 years ago

The black pottery high-handle cup unearthed at the Longshan Culture Relics dating back about 4,000 years ago. As this kind of black pottery is bright and as thin as eggshell, it is called "eggshell pottery".

The black writing ink we use today is mostly in liquid form, but in the old time writing ink was in the shape of rectangular or round sticks which produces black writing ink after being rubbed on ink stone with water.

The black writing ink used in Chinese calligraphy should occupy the highest position among all things black in the Chinese history, especially in Chinese culture. For thousands of years, the Chinese used ink brush with black ink to write and paint. Ancient Chinese scholars deemed the black ink stick as one of the four treasures in the study (the other three are the writing brush, ink grinding stone and paper).

The black writing ink must be coupled with the ink brush to produce works of calligraphic art. Manipulating the ink brush with black ink liquid absorbed by the brush tip may produce prized works of calligraphy, which through the centuries has become a unique art. And calligraphy remains a branch of art in China today, an art that boasts the greatest number of professionals and amateurs among all artistic forms in this country.

The characters of the Chinese written language are entirely different from the letters and words of the written languages of the Western world in their structures. The Chinese characters which number tens of thousands differ from one another in structure and the Chinese calligraphic art encompasses strokes of varying shapes and degrees of strength, the varying shapes of the characters, the combinations of the characters of strokes of different thicknesses and different sizes of characters in each column or row and the harmonious formations of the columns or rows and the composition of the characters in a whole page.

Accomplished calligraphers all strive to achieve the highest degree of artistic beauty and artistic styles of their own in each stroke of a character, each character in a column and each column in a page and the composition of a whole page or sheet. The Chinese calligraphic art falls into different schools and styles, being elegant and refined, or vigorous and untrammeled, or spontaneous and flowing, or elaborate and delicate.

永和九年歲在癸丑暮春之初會于會稽山陰之蘭亭脩禊事也群賢畢至少長咸集此地有崇山峻領茂林脩竹又有清流激湍暎帶左右引以為流觴曲水

The water-ink painting is a branch of the traditional Chinese painting. It is done entirely with the black ink, but executed in the full spectrum of blackness ranging from very black to varying degrees of gray. It is known generally that this style of black ink painting first appeared in the Tang Dynasty (618–907) and artists of this school hold that "the black is color and the black ink produces a multitude of colors." The mastery of the full spectrum of blackness enables the artist to bring out objects on the paper in dimensions and perspective, the shades of light, and the qualitative differences of the material of the objects. That is why traditional Chinese painters believe in the saying that "blackness without colors is more expressive than colors."

Although painters occasionally apply very light colors to their water-ink paintings, black color still dominates the works. The magic variations of black hues and symbolic approaches of the water-ink paintings are capable of bringing out the charm and flavor of the artistic works which ancient Chinese scholars described as "the charm of the ink." Wang Wei (701–761), the famous poet and painter of the Tang Dynasty, was the first to point out that "the water and ink constitute the highest of paintings." In the succeeding centuries, the form of water-ink paintings has remained the favorite of Chinese scholars who believe that this form of art has rendered the spontaneity of Nature in artistic creation. In their eyes, the blackness of Chinese writing ink on the white paper suffices to depict everything in the universe. To them, "the beauty of simplicity is supreme and peerless."

Mountains in Lanrong painted by Dong Qichang (1555–1636)

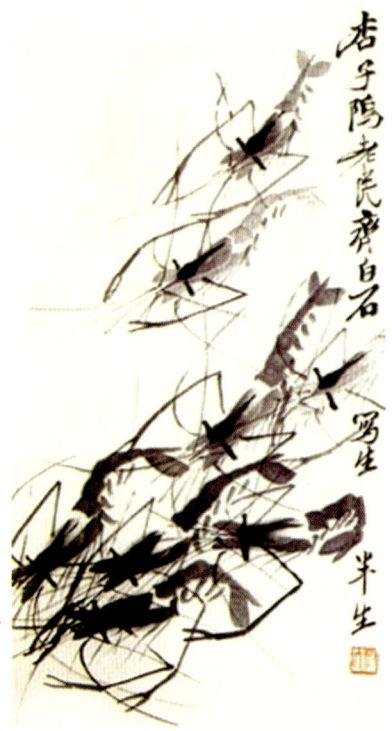

Prawns painted by Qi Baishi (1864–1957)

◀ Preface for the *Collection of Orchid Pavilion Poems* written by Wang Xizhi (303-361)

Special patterns sketched on the face of opera figures with certain colors are called "Opera mask" in China. The Peking Opera has more than 1,000 kinds of masks. It can be divided into red, purple, white, yellow, black, blue and green according to the main color of the face. Different colors with different connotations are painted in different patterns to symbolize different identities and characteristics of the roles.

Black facial mask is generally used for a character with moral integrity, honesty and bravery. Among the facial masks of Peking Opera, the most famous black face figure is Bao Zheng. Bao was a real person in Chinese history. He lived in the Northern Song Dynasty (960–1127). As an official, he was never afraid of power and position. He upheld justice and was impartial and incorruptible. He was honored as "Upright Official Bao" by Chinese people.

The Zhuang ethnic minority has most population among the minorities in China. Among the 12 branches of the Zhuang nationality, one of them is called "Black-clothes Zhuang". It is said that during a war in ancient times, this branch blackened their hands, faces and clothes with dyes made of indigo as their mark and finally won the war. Since then, the custom of wearing black clothes is handed down from generation to generation. They also gained their name "Black-clothes Zhuang".

COLORFUL CHINA

Miao nationality men are blowing *lusheng*, a reed-pipe wind instrument. They usually wear black and blue clothing, with black scarves wrapped around the head.

Yi nationality girls at Liangshan, Sichuan Province. The nationality mainly dwells in Yunnan, Sichuan, Guizhou and Guangxi. It is an ethnic that upholds black. Their clothes are mainly in black or dark blue.

A Yao nationality girl in splendid attire

Miao nationality girls

◀ Dong nationality girls

Chapter on White

White, the reflection of all visible colors on an object, is recognized universally as a color of purity and brightness.

The color of white has attained its profound cultural connotations with the passage of time over the centuries. The pure Xuan paper, translucent jade, beautiful white porcelain — all of them have left their lasting impressions of white on the traditional Chinese culture.

Out of religious belief or folk customs, white is the color upheld by many ethnic minorities such as Tibetan, Hui, Mongolian and Bai. These ethnic nationalities regard white as the embodiment of justice, loftiness and auspiciousness. Showing respects to white makes up an important part of their daily life and social culture. Yet, in the traditional customs of the Han people, white, in many occasions, indicates exhaustion and colorless and lifeless sign. It is a symbol of bad omen and sorrow. In many places, people believe red is for happiness while white is for mourning. In a mourning ceremony, people use white to express their sorrow. Therefore, in some happy occasions, white is a taboo that is shunned by people. However, along with the changes of time, such a concept has been fading.

COLORFUL CHINA

The snow-white world

A village in Northern China in winter

COLORFUL CHINA

The glaciers at Qinghai-Tibet Plateau

Qomolangma Peak straddles the border between China and Nepal. It is 8844.43 meters above the sea level, the highest peak in the world.

COLORFUL CHINA

Archeological findings show that paper was invented first in the Western Han period (206 BC –AD 25). The technique of paper making was ultimately spread from China to Korea, Japan, India, the Arab world and then by way of Africa to Europe. Hence, paper making has been recognized as one of the four major Chinese inventions in the world history of civilization.

The technology of making Xuan paper took place during the Tang Dynasty, marking the peak of the traditional paper making industry. Xuan paper is particularly suitable for writing and painting with the Chinese black ink and ink brush, for the paper is of special texture which is fine, tender, smooth and tenacious as people praise it as "a paper of longevity." The manufacture of Xuan paper has to go through more than 140 processes. It remains to be made manually even today.

Some assert that without Xuan paper, there is no way to appreciate the artistic charm of the traditional Chinese calligraphy and paintings. When writing or painting on Xuan paper with the traditional Chinese ink brush, Chinese calligraphers and painters are capable of creating strokes and splashes of ink of varying degrees of thickness, dry or wet texture and depths and perspectives by maintaining different ratio of water and ink and varying speed of the strokes to create different results of their artistic creation.

What is more important is the whiteness of the paper and the blackness of ink executed in an ideal combination and coordination to bring out the best images and vividness on paper. Chinese painters of the traditional school are very good at leaving untouched spaces on the paper to give viewers sufficient room for imagination. For instance, the white space at the back of flying birds denotes the sky and the space in which fish swims conveys the idea of water. In short, the unpainted blank spaces of a traditional painting can provide the infinite space of universe. Viewers may be caused to imagine hills and rivers, birds and blossoms out of the white spaces on the Xuan paper paintings.

Herding Buffalo painted by Li Keran (1907–1989). In the painting, two buffalos take a rest in water. The painter does not draw a line but keep the space in blank to leave a sense of ripples to people.

Kwan-yin Statue, white porcelain, Dehua Kiln, Fujian, Ming Dynasty

Children's pillow, white porcelain, Northern Song Dynasty

China is the hometown of porcelain. In the thousands of years, the porcelain industry in China has undergone three stages of development, namely, the stage of green porcelain (known in the West as celadon), that of white porcelain and that of painted porcelain. The onset of white porcelain served as a transitional period. White porcelain was developed on the basis of green porcelain and the success of white porcelain paved the way for the later development of brightly painted porcelain under or over the glaze.

Chinese white porcelain is entirely free from other colors. In addition to the quality of glaze, masters rely on innovations in shaping and other decorative skills to make their products attractive. The most exquisite white articles which have been preserved up to this day make people marvel at the richness of imagination of the masters in the designing of shapes and elaborate decorations purely in white on the base and glaze of the porcelain products of superb quality. The mono-color of white can arouse infinite aesthetic admiration instead of monotony. This simplicity of the Chinese white porcelain has a glamour of its own, a glamour borrowed from Nature.

"Blanc de China" was how French people lovingly called the Chinese white porcelain produced in Dehua Kiln in the Ming Dynasty (1368–1644). Chinese people called the white porcelain from Dehua Kiln "the ivory white" to describe the mellow look of white. The white porcelain of Dehua Kiln should represent the highest accomplishment of traditional Chinese white porcelain.

In the eyes of people of the Western world, jade is no more than a type of stone. But in the Chinese eyes, jade is unique for it has long transcended the concept of a mineral and become a carrier of a national mood. Since the beginning of the Chinese civilization, the love and admiration for jade has been deeply rooted in the hearts of the Chinese people.

Ancient Chinese began using jade articles as early as the Paleolithic Age some ten thousand years ago. Late in the Neolithic Age roughly 4,000 to 7,000 years ago, Chinese people used precious jade to make sacrificial utensils for paying homage to their ancestors and gods.

People's love for jade further deepened following the rise of the Confucian culture in China. Confucius (551–479 BC), the founder of Confucianism, personally believed that jade had the qualities of benevolence, wisdom, righteousness and propriety and that "a gentleman would never quit jade without reason." Gentlemen adorned themselves with jade ornaments not for decoration but as a reminder of the fine qualities in conduct and language. This idea has elevated the Chinese people's adoration for jade to a new height.

Of all jade stones, the white jade is most beloved by the Chinese people for its purity and fine quality. In the Chinese eyes, this whiteness best represents the mildness and loyalty and elegance and grace in the temperament of the gentleman. Other than the blue jade and yellow jade, white jade possesses the cultural character and moral quality upheld by the Chinese people.

The best white jade comes from Hetian of the Xinjiang Uygur Autonomous Region generally by the name of "Khotan jade". It is obtained from rocks that have fallen off the mountains ranging 3,500 to 5,000 meters above the sea level. The rocks rolled down the mountain slopes and after being washed by rain over long years broke into small pieces and were washed down to rivers. Khotan jade is white and the best Khotan jade attains a high degree of purity without the slightest flaw in it. It is so fine and soft looking that it resembles a piece of goat fat.

Jade pot of the Qing Dynasty (1644–1911)

For an outsider, Peking Opera mask is a mystery, but for Peking Opera fans, they can tell which character it is and which highlights it is from by taking a look at the mask. At least, they can tell whether it is a loyal, wicked, kind or evil one.

If an actor coming to the stage with a white face, it is needless to say that it is a wicked character. For example, the historical character Cao Cao (155–220) belongs to a wicked hero so that his mask uses white to indicate his treacherous and doubtful disposition.

At the Peking Opera stage, the faces of some performers are painted with a small piece of white. Whenever the fans see it, they know immediately that the character is a clown. As the saying goes, "there will be no opera if there is no clown." The role of clown is a major character in Peking Opera. The mask with a small piece of white, in way of cartoon, swiftly expresses the comic characteristics of this type of people.

COLORFUL CHINA

Entering Tibet, one enters a world with white as a major color. Even if it is in summer, the Himalaya Mountains in the southern part of the plateau and the Gangdise Mountains in the northern part of the plateau will be capped with snow, let alone the long winter. The main food for Tibetan people, roasted barley flour and shortening is white; the milk and barley wine is white. The shirts and sheepskin coats are white; the tents are mostly white and most of the external walls of the residential houses are painted with white. The gate of the house is usually painted with auspicious white patterns. The white sutra streamers and white Buddhist pagodas are seen everywhere…

The holy and pure snow-capped mountain

    White is a color worshipped by Tibetan people. It is a symbol of justice, kindness, loftiness, purity and auspiciousness. On occasions of greeting guests, visiting the senior people or showing respect to Buddha, the Tibetan people will usually present a white *hada*, a long piece of silk used as a greeting gift among the Tibetan people, to express their sincere and pure wishes. When drinking and having fun, some white sheep's wool will be hung on the handle of the pot. When a girl is to get married, she needs to ride on a white horse to show auspiciousness. When a family member passes away, a route will be sketched with white barley flour to guide the deceased into the heaven. People who spin the pray wheels find a piece of white cobblestone on their way, they will automatically pick it up and put it at a high place because they believe the white stones are holy stones.

Tibetan girls. White dresses are very popular with Tibetan people.

The white sutra streamers

The white Buddhist pagodas

"White moon and white elder sister, wearing a white shirt and white-cloth shoes and drape a white sheep skin…"

This is a popular song among Bai nationality people. It describes the ideal image of a girl. Judging from the words of the song, the nationality loves white.

Bai people inhabit Dali Bai Nationality Autonomous Prefecture in Yunnan. In their eyes, white is a symbol of purity and beauty. It also indicates auspiciousness, kindness and filial piety.

The dominant theme of the accessories of the Bai nationality is usually white from head to foot. Men's headcovering, women's head accessories and trousers are all white. On one side of the head accessories of an unmarried girl, there are long and white tassels. When a daughter of Bai nationality is to get married, the parents will place four dolomite stones at the corners of the dowry suitcase. It is said that such a marriage will be steady and the couple will get a baby at an earlier time. Among the dowries, there is usually a piece of complete white sheep skin. This is what the parents hope that the daughter will bring the virtue of hardworking and plain living to the in-laws.

On the vast expanse of Inner Mongolia grassland in Northern China, there live the nomadic Mongolians. Under the blue sky and white clouds, the vast grassland is dotted with purely white yurts. The white sheep scatter all over like pearls. White is considered the mother of everything by the Mongolians. It is a symbol of purity, loftiness, auspiciousness and happiness. The love and admiration of white is often seen in their daily life.

For Mongolians, the "white stuff" (various dairy products) is the most favorite food. On birthdays or trips, senior people will present the snow-white milk for a blessing ceremony.

"White Festival" is the most important holiday for Mongolians in a year. It is also called "White Moon". In some areas inhabited by Mongolians, the ancient customs of wearing white robes and presenting white gifts to express auspiciousness still remain.

At the Mongolian wedding ceremony, white is considered a symbol of auspiciousness. When the bridegroom welcomes the bride, he should wear a white belt on the waist and drink a bowl of fresh milk together with the bride. At the ceremony, the host will put the hands of both the bridegroom and the bride into a white cloth pocket and ask them to take a bow to people together. The new yurt for the newly weds is also covered with white stuff to express the congratulations.

COLORFUL CHINA

White is treated as a color of sacredness by Muslims. Legend has it that Mohammed, the founder of Islam has indoctrinated the believers: "You should often wear white clothes, as white clothes are most saintly and beautiful."

In China, Hui, Uygur, Kazak and other 10 ethnic minorities believe in Islam. Chinese male Muslims often wear white shirts and white caps, and female Muslims often wrap their heads in white scarves.

The Koreans in China mainly live in the three northeastern provinces of Jinlin, Liaoning and Heilongjiang. Koreans used to wear white clothes, addressing each other as "kinsman (woman) in white".

COLORFUL CHINA

In the traditions of the Han nationality and other nationalities in China, white, on one hand, has the meaning of purity. On the other hand, white is regarded as a taboo color in many occasions. It is a symbol of death, bad omen and sorrow. People call funeral affairs "white affairs". For funeral arrangements, the mourning hall is decorated with white. White sheet of silk bearing elegy and elegiac couplets are hung in the hall as white candles are burning. The family members of the deceased will wear white clothes, white hats and flowers. During the funeral procession, people will hold white streamers and litter white paper money.

Today, in many places, particularly in cities, people gradually get accustomed to use black to express their sorrow: Wearing black clothes, putting on a black mourning band on the arm. Besides, the elegiac couplets in the mourning hall are also in black. Yet, in rural areas, the tradition of using white for funeral affairs still remains unchanged.

Before the 20th century, aside from some ethnic minority areas, red was the main color at a wedding ceremony in China. The next choice of color is yellow. But white is a taboo. Even in other days, especially in festivals, people generally avoid wearing white clothes for fear of unluckiness.

For weddings, Chinese people use red and for mourning, Chinese people use white. The two colors are clearly divided. In early 20th century, when some people introduced the Western-style wedding ceremony into China, the white wedding garment was strongly reprimanded and objected. How could such an inauspicious color become the main role in a wedding? The white wedding garment was therefore once only popular in large cities. Most bridegrooms and brides completed their wedding ceremonies under the overwhelming red.

It is not until in recent 20 years, white wedding garment is gradually accepted by Chinese. In today's wedding ceremony, most brides will give priority in choosing white wedding garment that symbolizes purity and sacredness.

The Way of Black and White

Black and white, the two extremes on the spectrum, are deemed the ultimate abstraction of colors. Any color may approach either of the two extremes on the rise or fall in brightness. Black and white are opposites in unity, reaching the ultimate destination from different routes, which happens to conform to the world outlook of the ancient Chinese.

The Chinese knew colors early. But Lao Zi (circa 571–471 BC), the founder of Taoism, however, says: "The five colors blind people." The sage adds: "Humans follow the Earth, the Earth follows the Heaven, the Heaven follows the Tao, and the Tao follows Nature." What he intends to say is that human beings should comply with the Earth and the Heaven and be in harmony with Nature. Nature divides dark night from bright daytime. Therefore only the two colors of black and white are the natural colors of the Earth and Heaven which soothe the eye and rectify the mind.

Perhaps it is precisely because of that thinking that the two colors of black and white make their frequent presence in the traditional Chinese culture, such as the Chinese calligraphy, traditional Chinese water-ink paintings, the white walls and black tiles of traditional Chinese houses, etc. One artist once said: "The combination of the ink brush, black ink and paper, the three elements of traditional Chinese painting, has produced a perfect typical system of black and white. This system has been a unique and great contribution which the Chinese nation has made to the world art."

The forests in the mountains in Northern China in winter are just like a natural black and white water-ink painting.

COLORFUL CHINA

The black-and-white, charmingly naive giant panda is a rare animal in China. It is called by the Chinese as "national treasure".

Giant panda is the ancient extinct life as dinosaur. More than 3 million years ago, their footprints reached most places in southern and central parts of China as well as Myanmar and Vietnam. Due the strong geological and weather changes, other animal species of the time went distinct early and late. Giant panda was the only survivor and thus became a precious "living fossil".

Currently, the number of giant pandas living in the wild worldwide is a little more than 1,500. They live in the valleys of high mountains in Sichuan, Shaanxi and Gansu in China. China has now set up 59 giant panda natural reserves to effectively protect the wild giant panda species.

Red-crowned crane is almost purely white. The neck, part of its feather and feet are black, giving a sense of elegance and nobleness.

Among the more than 1,200 red-crowned cranes in the world, nearly two-thirds are in China. In Zhalong of Heilongjiang, Xianghai of Jilin in Northeast China and in Yancheng of East China, there are special preservation zones for the animals under first-class national protection.

In ancient China, people call the red-crowned crane as "immortal crane". In many popular legends, when a person became an immortal, he or she would ride on an immortal crane. As the life span of the red-crowned crane can be as long as 60 years, it leads a long life among the birds. It is regarded as a symbol of longevity and auspiciousness. It is always mentioned together with pine trees. When Chinese people congratulate on the birthday of senior people, they often say *song he yannian*, meaning the life will be as long as the pines and cranes. The painting of pine trees and cranes has always been a familiar gift to congratulate senior people's birthday.

COLORFUL CHINA

Hongcun Village in Yixian County, Anhui Province, is honored as the "rural village in Chinese painting".

    The combination of white walls and black tiles constitutes the most common scene in Southern China, especially the area in the southern part of the Yangtze River Delta.

    Walking in many ancient townships in the southern part of the Yangtze River Delta, the white-wall and black-tile civilian residential houses are all in sight. The black and white are well arranged to match the small bridge and flowing water as well as the long and quiet lanes.

    The Huizhou area by the side of Xinanjiang River at the foot of the Huangshan in southern Anhui Province is known for its well-preserved Ming and Qing Dynasty civilian residential compounds. The Huizhou architecture gives people the deepest impression of the harmony of black and white. Every simple building there has a slope roof and its corresponding "horse-head" wall to form a black surface and line to set off the large space of white wall. The white walls and black tiles serve as a foil to the surrounding mountains and water. Looking from afar, it is just like a scroll of water-ink painting inlaid in the green mountains and water.

    The white wall of the civilian residential houses in Huizhou was not seeking for the aesthetics at the beginning. It was built to prevent dampness and reflect the sunshine. Later, as the local culture developed, particularly affected by the Chinese water-ink painting, this kind of quiet, simple and elegant beauty, the harmony with natural surroundings of the black and white gained more and more recognitions from people.

Zhouzhuang, a water-town in Jiangsu Province

Diagram of *Taiji*

The most classic combination of black and white should be the diagram of *Taiji*. (in Chinese meaning the ultimate or the very origin, or the very beginning of the universe). *Taiji* is a very important concept in the Chinese ideological history, which illustrates the course of the emergence of the universe, the inception and evolution of things. The ancient Chinese believed that the way of Nature was the creation of everything through the combination of *yin* and *yang*. Therefore in their view, the boundless universe and everything in it were characterized by the mutually opposite and mutually reliant two aspects of *yin* and *yang*.

The eight trigrams of the *Taiji* Diagram formed by the two colors of black and white are capable of comprehensively interpreting the unique world outlook of the ancient Chinese. An S-shaped line divides up a circle into a black half and a white half, the white of which represents *yang* and the black of which represents *yin*, with a black dot in the white half and a white dot in the black half to show *yang* contains the element of *yin* and *yin* contains the element of *yang*. Black and white, *yin* and *yang*, thus integrate into one. Meanwhile, the two serve as the root of each other in a perpetual cycle of evolution and mutual transformation.

The seeming simplicity of black and white combination actually embraces the way of everything in the universe. Black represents *yin* whereas white represents *yang*; white means the Heaven and black means the Earth; white stands for reality and black stands for abstraction; white means movement whereas black means stillness; white is the positive and black is the negative; white embodies masculinity whereas black embodies femininity … All things ultimately boil down to black and white, which in the eyes of ancient Chinese philosophers were no longer just two colors, but the essence of the universe and life.

Practicing Tai Chi Chuan

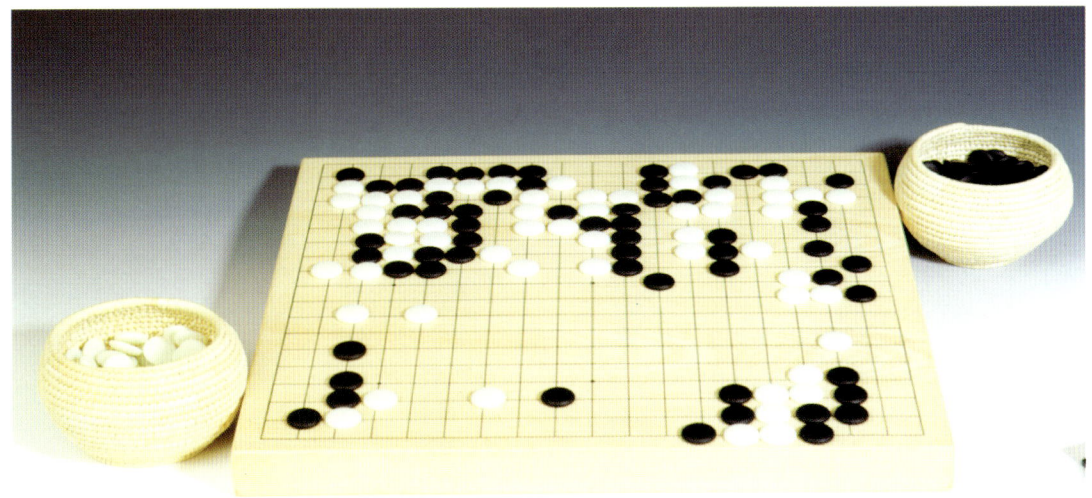

Black and white in its relationship with the universe and life find their vivid expression in the traditional Chinese chess game *weiqi* (the Japanese call it *go*).

The game is played by two persons, with one playing the white pieces and the other playing the black pieces by way of representing *yang* and *yin*. The chess board is divided into 361 intersections formed by 19 horizontal lines and 19 vertical lines. The moment the first piece is placed on the board, a game of the birth and evolution of a new world unfolds. The games develops with white and black pieces on the board placed one by one by the players alternately in a fashion of continuous changes of the situation denoting the mutation of the forces of *yin* and *yang* in the universe. The game of continuous changes of the strengths of the two sides, denotes the changes of the *yin* and *yang* strengths of the *Taiji* Diagram with infinite variations.

An old saying in China goes: "The Heaven serves as the chess board and the stars are the chess pieces." The game of *weiqi* in fact is the universe in miniature and the way of the game is the way of the Heaven, the way of the Earth and the way of humanity. Therefore playing *weiqi* is not just a game of intelligence but also held as a way of character cultivation and wisdom enlightenment. The goal of *weiqi* chess is not the gain or loss of some pieces; it is deemed a world of opposites in unity comprising the black and white pieces. A *weiqi* master is good at understanding the functions of the white and black pieces, mastering the rules governing the changes of the development of the game and maintaining an equilibrium of forces. The changing situation of the chess game very much resembles the way of life to a person. By grasping the spirit of *weiqi* game, one may grasp the way of life, gain the wisdom of taking optimum steps in the light of reality and dawn on the truth of life and the universe.

Chapter on
Gray

Gray, a transitional color of varying degrees between black and white, is more concealed, subtle, blurred, and low-keyed than black. It is also more flexible, potentially more powerful and tenacious than black.

The Chinese people are best knowledgeable with gray, which has virtually stemmed from the color of tiles and bricks of traditional Chinese buildings.

Stones in the nature are mainly gray. Chinese people have a special feeling toward stones.

It can be found in the Chinese landscape paintings that people show favor to peaks with many stones. Yet the beautiful stones in the nature are usually far away from the cities and towns. It is impossible for people to see them everyday. Therefore, people move these stones into gardens so that they can appreciate anytime. In Chinese classic gardens, it is often seen a view of a piece of stone or an artificial mountain with piled-up stones either in front of or behind a hall or by the side of a pond on the wall corner. Most of these stones are in unprocessed natural shape. They are tall and straight and delicately shaped. With the smart arrangement and combination of the builder, the stones boast graceful bearing but natural.

Most men of letters in history loved stones. Some called the stone as brother or teacher and some slept by holding a stone. They gave more life and intelligence to the stones. Among the four classic books in ancient China, *Journey to the West* and *Dream of Red Mansions*, their main characters incarnated from stone. The first name of *Dream of Red Mansions* was *Stories of Stones*.

◀ Huangshan Mountain in Anhui Province is often said of "no peak being not of a stone and no stone not having a story." Its unique and exquisite peaks have become the most common topic for landscape painting by scholars in history.

The rockery in Chinese gardens is just like a naturally made abstract sculpture, leaving people unlimited space for imagination.

Yungang Grottoes in Shanxi Province. The stelae and sculptures made of stone can be found all over China.

The stone house of Buyi nationality in Guizhou Province. Traditional Chinese architecture is mostly made of wooden structure. Stone houses are usually seen as residence of minority nationalities.

COLORFUL CHINA

In ancient China, city wall was the most important military defense work of a city. When building a city in the past, the planner would channel enormous human power and financial support to the city wall. The length, height and width of the city wall and the number and size of tower and battlement on the wall all reflected the grade and the importance of defense of a city.

Before the Song Dynasty (960–1279), the walls were piled up with stones or rammed with earth. With the invention of gunpowder and its wide application in attacking cities, it became common that city walls were covered or laid with bricks. These building materials made the city walls look gray.

Relatively complete and well-preserved ancient city wall is not much now. The famous ancient city walls are seen in Xi'an, Shaanxi Province, Nanjing, Jiangsu Province and Pingyao, Shanxi Province.

The ancient city wall of Pingyao, Shanxi Province, has a history of more than 600 years.

The ancient city wall of Xi'an, Shaanxi Province, was first built in the 1370s.

COLORFUL CHINA

The pit of terra-cotta warriors and horses at the Tomb of Emperor Qinshihuang in Xi'an, Shaanxi Province is honored as the No. Eighth Miracle in ancient civilization in the world.

Emperor Qinshihuang (259–210 BC), the first emperor of the Qin Dynasty (221–206 BC), established the first centralized feudal country in the Chinese history and gained the title of "First Emperor in History". His tomb consumed massive engineering and took 39 years and more than 700,000 workers at most to complete. The excavated part includes more than 600 accompanying pits and tombs. Among them, the most famous one is the widely known terra-cotta warriors and horses.

Today, when visitors enter the excavated sites of terra-cotta warriors and horses, they will see thousands of gray pottery warriors and horses standing in order to form a huge military array, giving a stirring solemnity and awe. The warrior is generally 1.8 meters tall and the horse is 1.5 meters tall. Surprisingly, there are no warriors of the same looking, posture and expression. From the structure of the body to hairs, eyebrows and shoelaces are all carefully carved.

In fact, when these pottery figures were first made and buried, they were painted with various wonderful colors. It was because of fire burn, soaked in water and other reasons the colors faded and turned to be the current gray array.

The Great Wall stretches thousands of miles to the Far West of China, crawling on top of the ridges of mountains and crossing grasslands and Gobi deserts. As a symbol of China, the Great Wall, too, is gray in color.

The gigantic project of building the Great Wall lasted from the 7th century B.C. through the 17th century under a dozen feudal regimes. According to the calculations by some scholars, the combined length of the Great Wall constructed in the more than two thousand years should add up to more than 50,000 kilometers, which, together with the numerous fortresses at frontier passes, commanding forts and smoke towers, formed into a relatively comprehensive military defense system. The Great Wall we see today is virtually what was restored or rebuilt during the Ming Dynasty.

The construction of the Great Wall reflected different engineering technologies and technical levels at different periods of time. However, despite the variety of the features in engineering, the entire Great Wall has maintained its uniformity of the color of gray, thanks to the similarity of the materials used.

Today when we touch the old gray bricks of the Great Wall with our fingers, our thought cannot but drift to the fierce battles and the bloodbaths over the wall of the bygone days. The Great Wall no doubt is a miracle in the world history of engineering. But behind this miracle has been an untold record of consumption of manpower, money and material over a very long period of more than two millennia. Every section of the Great Wall performed the same mission — to ward off war. The bricks piled up one by one with so much sweat and blood in the long years should have borne a simple and plain aspiration of a nation — the aspiration for peace!

COLORFUL CHINA

Should you stand on top of the Jingshan Hill behind the Imperial Palace in Beijing 20 years ago, you would have had a panoramic view of tiled roofs of varying shades of gray of this ancient capital city arranged neatly into rectangular plots each comprising a number of courtyard compounds, with only the red-walled Imperial Palace buildings with yellow-glazed tiles standing out in the center. Despite the fast paced urban construction in recent two decades and the loss of that nostalgic panorama, Beijing still retains many gray back lanes and courtyard compounds serving as a landmark reminder of the ancient capital and its traditional architectural culture.

The courtyard compound, as its name indicates, is a walled compound with houses erected on all four sides linked up by corridors to form a central courtyard. Courtyard compounds however differ vastly. The most gorgeous and largest were the mansions of the imperial princes and other aristocrats, which may each

Beijing lanes under the shade of trees

contains a chain of seven to nine courtyards or just a small single courtyard dwelled by a common family. One feature of Beijing lanes is that they are lined by courtyard compounds on both sides and one could hardly give an exact number of Beijing's lanes which are locally called by the Mongolian pronunciation of "hutong".

The gray brick walls and gray roof tiles are ordinary and plain almost to the extreme, but they render the dwellings a feeling of spontaneity and sobriety. Inside the gray walled compounds, however, are small worlds bubbling with vitality. Old Beijing residents are all familiar with the old saying: "The reed awnings, fish jars and pomegranate trees; old men, fat dogs and sweet maids" — a vivid picture of old Beijing courtyard compound! The gray courtyard compound houses in the quiet *hutongs* have bred vigorous lives in a subdued way, which mirrors the quality of simplicity and sobriety of the traditional Beijing life.

Courtyard compound is a common style for civilian residential house in northern cities in China. Courtyard compound at Pingyao, Shanxi Province, also has gray bricks and tiles.

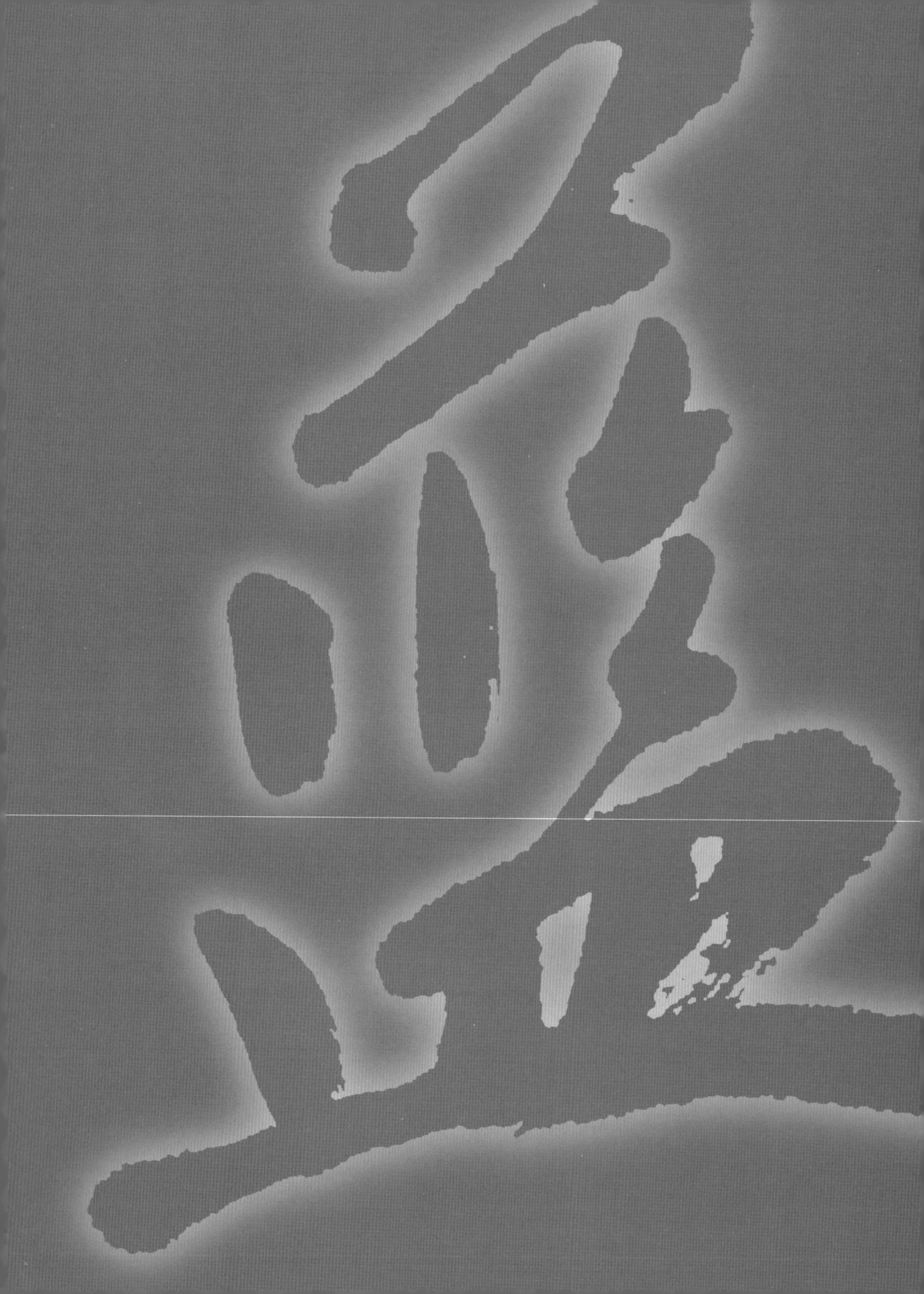

Chapter on Blue

The sky where birds fly is blue and the sea where ships swim is blue. The sky and the sea are so far and wide that they all look blue and profound. Blue is a color of vastness and profundity.

In the traditional Chinese culture, however, blue is a color without much obvious connotation. Yet that background has not prevented the color of blue to exert its particular charm on the ancient soil of China. The porcelain with blue floral patterns represents grace and elegance. The indigo print cotton cloth has a plain beauty. The blue glassworks show transparence of blue. The blue of cloisonne products has its special glamour of attractive and profound blue. Those things in blue color with different features of their own have been embellishing the lives of the Chinese people and nourishing their minds.

COLORFUL CHINA

Blue is the color of the sky. It might be human being's most primitive and lasting impression of the color.

Legendary story in China has it that in the earliest time, the heaven and the earth was connected and everything was in chaos. Later, Pan Gu separated the earth from heaven with big axes and then human beings were born.

In ancient China, the unlimited and everlasting "Heaven" has always been the highest deities worshipped by people. The rulers also used "Heaven" to prove their legitimism. Imperial emperors in the Chinese history claimed themselves the "son of Heaven" and they received mission from "Heaven" and helped the "Heaven" to rule the country and manage ordinary people. In all the sacrificial ceremonies, offering sacrifices to Heaven was the most important. The emperor was the only person qualified for the ceremony.

The Chinese mainland borders on Bohai Sea, Yellow Sea, East China Sea and South China Sea in the east and south. It has a sea area of 4.73 million square kilometers. Its coastal line is about 18,000 kilometers. Within its waters, there are 5,400 islands.

COLORFUL CHINA

Namco Lake in Tibet is 4,718 meters above the sea level. It is the highest saltwater lake in the world. In Tibetan language, Namco means "Heavenly lake". It is a sacred land for Tibetan Buddhism. Buddhist believers from all over the Tibetan area will come to worship and spin the prayer wheels along the lake.

Covering an area of 4,583 square kilometers, Qinghai Lake is the largest inland lake in China. It is also the largest saltwater lake in China. In Mongolian and Tibetan language, Qinghai Lake means "blue sea".

COLORFUL CHINA

Qinghua porcelain plate, Qing Dynasty

The generally known *Qinghua* porcelain of China is actually a white porcelain body painted with blue patterns in cobalt. This category of Chinese porcelain carries the most classic blue of the traditional Chinese art.

The porcelain is painted with blue floral patterns in cobalt on the surface of a white porcelain body and covered with a transparent layer of glaze before being fired at a temperature of around 1,300 degrees Celsius in kiln. The firing enables the cobalt pigment to penetrate into the paste to show charmingly blue color of varying thickness. The *Qinghua* porcelain was made first in the 13th century and became the mainstay of Chinese porcelain products during the three dynasties of Yuan, Ming and Qing.

The Chinese *Qinghua* porcelain conquered the world with its charming blue patterns on pure white ground as soon as it reached Europe. Today articles of the Chinese *Qinghua* porcelain ware are treasures kept in many of the most famous museums across the world. Westerners like to call the *Qinghua* porcelain simply as "Chinese porcelain" not only because the output of Qinghua porcelain was big, but because the charm of the blue floral patterns truly represents the subtlety and elegance of the Chinese aesthetic taste.

Compared with the white porcelain, the *Qinghua* porcelain with blue patterns in cobalt conveys a lasting charm; whereas in contrast to porcelain with colorful patterns, the blue patterns on a white background show a sober and quiet charm. Blue and white complement each other to convey a graceful taste characteristic of the Chinese traditional water-ink paintings.

Qinghua porcelain vase with patterns of seawater and dragon, Ming Dynasty

COLORFUL CHINA

A fairly short walk southward from the central Tiananmen Square at the middle of the Changan Boulevard in Beijing will bring you to a large group of buildings with shining glazed roofs of blue color. That is the Temple of Heaven, where the world's largest alter for paying homage to Heaven is located.

The Temple of Heaven was completed simultaneously with the Imperial Palace in 1420 after 14 years of construction. In all, twenty-three emperors of the Ming and Qing dynasties held sacrificial ceremonies there.

The Temple of Heaven covers an area of 2,730,000 square meters, as compared to the 720,000 square meters of the Imperial Palace. That was to show the emperor's esteem for the Heaven. All of the buildings in the Temple of Heaven followed the same architectural concept to show the supremacy of the Heaven.

All of the buildings are roofed with blue-glazed tiles to signify the heaven. The most brilliant of all is the Hall of Pray for Good Harvest, a round structure of three layers of eaves and the blue-glazed tiles shine brilliantly in the sun to give an air of supreme tranquility.

The hall was originally rectangular in shape and when it was rebuilt, it became the present round shaped and the three layers of glazed tiles were blue, yellow and green in color to signify the heaven, the earth and everything in between. Emperor Qianlong (reigned 1736–1795) of Qing ordered to have the color of the tiles changed all into blue in 1751. Every time when the emperor officiated over the ceremony, he had to change from his yellow dragon robe into a blue robe to show his utmost respect for the God of Heaven.

COLORFUL CHINA

The blue glazed dragon at the Nine-Dragon Wall in the Imperial Palace, Beijing

Blue glazed plate, Tang Dynasty

Cloisonne is a kind of traditional Chinese handicraft art. A cloisonne article is made with a floral pattern or other design on the ground of a copper vase or any other article by applying color enamel in the tiny sockets created by a filigree pattern inlaid on the copper base.

Cloisonne should be considered partially introduced from abroad, for the handicraft art of using enamel was first introduced into China from Persia late in the 14th century. Chinese handicraft masters developed filigree patterns inlaid on the base of copper of articles and filled with color enamel to create cloisonne. In the early days, blue was the dominating color in cloisonne articles. Now cloisonne articles are in all colors as a result of the development of the technological processes.

Cloisonne articles used to be owned exclusively by the imperial families and feudal lords as symbols of power and wealth. The most luxurious cloisonne articles were made entirely in gold base and gold filigree. Some of gold cloisonne articles of the Qing Palace are now on display in the Beijing Palace Museum and the Summer Palace, open to sightseers.

Today cloisonne as a handicraft art is still made manually. Cloisonne articles are no longer the monopoly of the imperial palace, but are available to ordinary people.

Cloisonne bottle

Cloisonne tea set

The indigo prints made by Bai nationality women

The small-peasant economy in old China was characterized by "men tilling the land and women spinning and weaving in every rural household." As early as during the Eastern Zhou period (770–256 BC), people already mastered the skill of using a certain plant to extract pigment to dye fabrics. For thousands of years, blue had remained as the principal color of the clothing of common people in China.

Cloth printed with indigo floral patterns first appeared about more than 1,300 years ago and its appearance immediately enlivened the blue cotton cloth. Blue cotton prints were used to make garments, bed covers, curtains, aprons, bags and other things. Prior to the modern machine printed cotton prints, the indigo prints had remained closely linked with the life of the ordinary Chinese people.

The base cloth of indigo prints is the home-spun cloth woven by country women. The motifs of the floral patterns are derived from inspirations nurtured by the countryside landscape, flowers, birds and beasts, and traditional theatrical images. The indigo prints with different motifs suit different occasions and represent the modest aspirations of Chinese country folks.

Pieces of indigo prints are hung out to dry in the sun after repeated rinsing.

The indigo prints might look boorish in contrast to soft silks, and it might be too modest in contrast to gorgeously colorful brocade. But that crudeness and rusticity possess a subtle quality of refinement and modesty with a lasting flavor for people to appreciate.

Worshipping habitation of spirits, a traditional activity to offer sacrifices to deities of the Mongolian people.

A Mongolian girl

Mongolian nationality mainly inhabit in Northern China. It is the largest nomadic nationality in China. Mongolians once called themselves "huhemenggule", meaning blue Mongolia.

The Heavenly blue is a symbol of endlessness, loyalty and faithfulness. In Mongolian language, many wonderful things are described with blue. For example, the capital of the Inner Mongolia Autonomous Region is called "Hohhot", which means a blue city. When giving a name to a child, many Mongolians love to put a prefix of "hoh", which means blue.

The Mongolian people love to wear blue garment. On many occasions such as receiving guests, visiting, birthday-congratulations, wedding banquet and sacrificing ceremonies, they will present a blue *hada*. The blue *hada* is not only a symbol of sacredness, endlessness, but also an auspicious blessing.

Miao nationality girls in festival costumes

Dong villagers sing toasting song for the guests from afar.

Lisu nationality men

Buyi nationality men and women sing in pairs.

Chapter on
Green.

Green as the basic color of Nature represents life, signifies health, and symbolizes peace. In the sober color of green, people inhale into their innermost the freshness of air and enjoy peace of mind.

Green being a favorite color to the Chinese people has much to do with the unique Chinese belief in the unity of Nature and humanity. The three major ideologies in China, Confucianism, Taoism and Buddhism, all emphasize the importance of integration of man with the Heaven and Earth and the pursuit of harmony and unity between humankind and Nature. Green, therefore, is a color deep-rooted in the hearts of the Chinese people.

The green mountains and rivers of the natural environment constitute the home of humankind, a home free from all worldly concerns. Green is also a perpetual theme to Chinese literature, paintings and other traditional Chinese arts. No matter whether it is a tall tree with a huge canopy or a blade of grass, lushly green bamboos or the tender budding leaves of tea shrubs, they all attract human beings to communicate with Nature in soul language and experience the superb state of mind in unity with it.

The Three-Gorges of the Yangtze River

Hulunbir Prairie in Inner Mongolia that covers about 100,000 square kilometers is the largest natural grassland in the world.

COLORFUL CHINA

Tianshan Mountain in the Xinjiang uygur Autonomous Region

Paddy fields in south of the Yangtze River

The ladder fields in the mountainous areas in Southern China

COLORFUL CHINA

The green of bronze ware is not the color of the ware itself, but the outcome of oxidization with the passage of long years. This green coating that has formed over probably thousands of years is by no means corrosive to the bronze object; rather it is a protective cover. This green cover records the old age of the bronze ware, conveying a profundity of history.

Bronze was the first metal mankind made extensive use in daily utensils in history. The civilization of bronze appeared not only in China, but also in Egypt and the Two-River Valley. But the Chinese bronze civilization was beyond comparison by its counterparts.

Bronze ware was the most outstanding ritual article among all ritual articles made of other materials in ancient China. The emperors and feudal lords made some large bronze ware for sacrificial ceremonies and state banquets, or even as symbols of state power. Bronze articles as ritual ware were used in accordance with rigid rules. The quantity, size and form of the bronze articles might vary strictly in compliance with the rank of the person officiating the event.

The bronze articles made prior to the Qin Dynasty also included weapons, in addition to ritual articles. After the Qin unified the whole of China, Emperor Qin Shihuang ordered all weapons in the country confiscated and amassed in Luoyang which were melted and cast into 12 giant bronze human figures. That is why much less bronze weapons than ritual articles have been unearthed from ancient tombs of the later periods.

With the arrival of the Iron Age after the Western Zhou period, the bronze culture declined gradually. But the Bronze Age occupies an extraordinary position in the Chinese history of the development of human civilization.

Bronze head sculpture, unearthed at Sanxingdui, Sichuan Province. Sanxingdui bronze is usually exaggerating in shape. It has great difference with the bronze from the central part of China.

A bronze of the Shang Dynasty (1600–1046 BC)

Colorful China

Between the 3rd century and the 6th century, the production of celadon became the rapidest developing handicraft in China. The Yue kiln of the Tang Dynasty, Longquan Kiln, Ru Kiln and Yaozhou Kiln of the Song Dynasty became famous kilns for producing celadon.

The beauty of celadon does not lay in the uniqueness of its shape or the complicated patterns but its gentle, subtle and restrained, reserved and elegant color. Some people use "the jade color of peaks" to refer the beauty of the glaze of celadon. Some people refer it as clear ripples of a lake. More people praise the jade-like color of its glaze. In the eyes of Chinese people, jade is the essence of the heaven, earth, sun and moon. The celadon with its color and sense of reality of jade will naturally win favor from people.

The green of celadon is gentle and clear. Through the jade-like green layer of glaze, one will feel the quiet, leisure and oriental elegance.

Jade stone is classified into hard stone and soft stone in China. Green jadeite is a kind of hard stone. The first batch of green jadeite was believed to be imported from Burma roughly in the 15th century when the white jade, blue jade and yellow jade popular in China at the time were all soft stone.

Green jadeite is mostly green, but there are also red, purple, blue, yellow, gray, white and other colors. And the green jadeite has varying degrees of depths of green. Generally the green jadeite with deep, even and translucent green is recognized as of a higher quality and priced higher.

The pursuit of green jadeite reached a high tide in the Qing Dynasty. The green jadeite imports from Burma provided an incessant flow of this precious stone into China. And ornaments of green jadeite were sought with great zeal by the imperial family and high ranking officials and wealthy people. Green jadeite was made into rings, necklaces, snuff-bottles, smoking pipe-heads, and beads of official necklaces of the Qing officials.

An old Chinese saying goes: "Without skillful carving, jade cannot become fine articles." So the processing of jade into exquisite articles and ornaments requires great skill and ingenious designing. This is equally important to the processing of green jadeite articles. The handicraftsmen have to make very clever and innovative designs to bring out the best on the basis of the different colors, veins and shapes of the material.

Green bamboos have been playing a very important part in the lives of the Chinese people since the ancient time. Dr. Joseph Needham has a terse term for China when he wrote: "This is a country of bamboos."

Bamboo culture is an important feature that has distinguished the Chinese culture from all other cultures. Chopsticks made of bamboo are the indispensable tools at meals; bamboo chariots used to be unique Chinese means of transportation; bamboo strips had played an important role in helping carry forward the Chinese culture; bamboo stems form part of the unique Chinese ink brushes; bamboo is made into Chinese flutes; poems on bamboo constitute an independent category of traditional Chinese poetry; and bamboo is an important motif of traditional water-ink paintings to express the modesty of the mind.

Bamboo in the eyes of the Chinese is also an embodiment of exemplary conduct and moral integrity. The Chinese deem bamboo plants to have the quality of modesty instead of vanity, straightforwardness and self-discipline instead of subservience and flattery, that they remain green the year round showing no fear for cold and wind.

Many learned people in ancient China loved to plant bamboos in their courtyards. They made friends with bamboos for they wished to withdraw from society and elevate their moral world above vulgarity. Su Dongpo (1037–1101), the great literary giant of the Song Dynasty, once said: "I can do without meat, but I cannot do without bamboos. Lack of meat may make one thin, but without bamboos, one will become vulgar."

COLORFUL CHINA

China, the homeland of tea, has been a forerunner of tea growing, processing and drinking. Chinese tea falls into six major categories of green tea, red tea, O Long tea, black tea, yellow tea and white tea, depending on different processing techniques. Among them, green tea has the longest history and leads all other categories in output. After green tea leaves are made into a drink by pouring in boiled water, the color of both water and tea leaves are green, hence its name.

Green tea is made to maintain its natural fresh aroma and flavor. It may taste very light at the first sipping, but the gentle flavor of green tea stays on the palate for a long time.

Modern laboratory analysis shows green tea has retained much of the natural elements which are believed to be helpful with curing inflammation, sterilizing, delaying aging and preventing and resisting malignant tumor.

When drinking green tea, a connoisseur does not drain the cup at one gulp, but takes the three steps of looking, sniffing, and tasting to see the color and shape of the tea leaves first, then to smell the aroma, and after waiting the leaves to stretch out and settle in the water, to sip the water slowly to savor the purity, spirit and beauty of tea.

Tea grows in mountains and thrives on the nourishment from Nature. Tea has to be processed by human wisdom. So we should try to squeeze time out of the bustle and hustle of our life, find a quiet corner, make a cup of tea and enjoy the mild aroma and flavor of tea all to your own or share your enjoyment with a few friends — just to relish on the nice feeling of the integration of man and Nature!

The green tea liquid

A tea garden

COLORFUL CHINA

In many places in China, the most common tree that is everlasting is pine tree. This ordinary plant will usually arouse much imagination of the Chinese people. In the poems and paintings in the past, people continued to recite and describe pine trees. It seems that they will never be tired of it. The evergreen of pine tree and its vigorous vitality on the infertile cliff have been transferred into a symbol of indomitable, persistent and loft personality. Among ordinary people, pine tree means longevity. People often say "your happiness will be like water in East China Sea that flows all the time and your life will be as young as the pine tree in the southern mountain" when congratulating people for birthday.

A Mosque in Turpan, the Xinjiang Uygur Autonomous Region

Nanguan Mosque in Yinchuan, the Ningxia Hui Autonomous Region

Green is regarded as a sacred color by Islamism. It is a symbol of life and hope.
In the middle of the 7th century when the Islamism was first established, it was spread into China from Arabian region. Among the 56 ethnic nationalities in China, 10 minorities such as Hui, Uygur, Kazak, Dongxiang, Kirgiz, Salar, Tajik, Uzbek, Bao'an and Tatar believe in Islamism.

The worship of green is reflected in the garment accessories, religious architecture and civilian residential houses of these nationalities. Uygur men love to wear green flowery hats. Many Hui women love to wear green head-cover. The doors, windows and walls of a Muslim family are all painted in green; the roof of the mosque is green; some even have green external wall; the carpet for people to pray in the mosque also has green background; the shops that sell Muslim food hang a sign with green background.

Chapter on Yellow

Yellow, the color of autumn leaves and ripe grain crops, is the most brilliant color of Nature, a color that signifies maturity and harvest.

In the Chinese version of Genesis, the God of Heaven created the ancestors of the Chinese nation with yellow clay. Dwelling on the Yellow River and on the Yellow Earth known as loess and propagating there, the Chinese people have formed an indissoluble bond with the color of yellow. Even the Chinese skin has attained the color of the loess plateau. The Chinese, an industrial, kind and tenacious people, have created a unique civilization in the world on this land of yellow color.

For a very long period of time in the Chinese history, however, the color of yellow was closely related to the supreme imperial power beyond the reach of the ordinary people. Yellow was symbolic of majesty and supremacy — a color with a measure of mystic power in the eyes of many people in China.

The paddy field with bumper harvest

Rape-seed flowers

Boatmen at the Yellow River

When we trace the origin of humanity, we find all of the major early human civilizations rose from the plains of river valleys, one of which was the ancient Chinese civilization. And the Yellow River Basin served as the cradle of that civilization. Archeological findings show that human lives could be traced back to more than a million years ago in the Yellow River Basin.

The Yellow River originates on the northern slope of the Bayan Har Mountain on the Qinghai-Tibet Plateau and meanders eastward for more than 5,400 kilometers. More than two thousand years ago, the Chinese people simply called the Yellow River "the River." The present name of the river was derived from the river water laden with heavy silt as a result of the water and soil erosion in the later years. Today the very mention of the Yellow River reminds people of the turbulent flow of the yellow water of the river.

The Yellow River Basin had been the political, economic and cultural center of China for thousands of years since Xia, the first dynasty of the recorded Chinese history 21 centuries before Christ, up to early 12th century. The ancient Chinese capitals in the Yellow River Basin include Xi'an, Luoyang, Kaifeng and Zhengzhou, all of which were nurtured by the water of the Yellow River.

Over the past tens of thousands of years, the Yellow River has brought blessings as well as troubles and disasters to the Chinese people in its basin. How to tame this unruly river has been a primary task for the rulers of numerous dynasties. The Chinese people are very familiar with the stories of the Great Yu and his father leading the people in taming the Yellow River. Legends say that Gun, Yu's father, tried to block the flooding water from the Yellow River and failed. The Great Yu directed people to guide the flooding water to the sea and succeeded. This story that reflects the wisdom of the philosophy of guidance instead of suppression remains the guiding thinking to the work of water conservancy today.

◀ The highest flow of Hukou Waterfall at the Yellow River can reach 8,000 cubic meters per second.

COLORFUL CHINA

The middle reaches of the Yellow River run through the world-known loess plateau, with its turbulent torrent draining an area of some 370,000 square kilometers mostly covered with a thick layer of loess, the greatest concentration of loess in the world. The silt washed off from the loess plateau turns the River into a yellow turbid flow.

The loess soil, loose and fertile, is ideal for farming, should there be a humid climate and good irrigation, which nurtured the early agricultural civilization of China. A very popular fairy tale among the Chinese people says that once upon a time there was a fairy named Nüwa who created a yellow human race with the yellow clay and water from the river. That race was the origin of the Chinese nation. Although merely a fairy tale out of sheer imagination, the story still shows how deep the Chinese nation has been rooted in the loess soil.

The loess plateau stretches with rolling hills and is cut by numerous gullies. Cave dwellings were dug into the slopes row by row, forming unique scenery on the plateau. The ruggedness of the environment has tempered a tenacious character of the local people. The people populated on the vast plateau today have carried on the carefree and dauntless character of their ancestors and retained the simplicity and tenacity of temperament stemming from the Yellow River and loess plateau. *Xin Tian You*, a folksong of the loess plateau, the title of which means "traveling without a definite destination," is a song of high pitch, simple lyric and most indigenous melody, best airs the fire-like fervor of the people on the rugged loess plateau.

COLORFUL CHINA

For more than a thousand years, the vast Gobi deserts in Northwest China were traversed by numerous camel caravans. The slow moving camels imprinted the boundless yellow sand their footsteps and the caravan bells under the necks of camels were heard ringing solitarily over the sand dunes. That picture of camel caravans moving along a route of the deserts cannot be deleted from the memories of people, historians and the common people alike. That route was the world-renowned Silk Road.

In the 2nd century before Christ, a trade channel between China and the West was opened, which started from Changan (Xi'an today), passed the Gansu Corridor and West Asia and reached Europe. Because the bulk of the merchandize China traded with the West were silk along that road, the German geographer Ferdinand von Richthofen later in the 19th century named that road the Silk Road.

From the 2nd century before Christ through the 13th century, the Silk Road was the principal channel for political, economic and cultural exchanges between China and the countries in the West. Merchants, envoys and monks trudged along the Silk Road. They had to travel through the rugged Takla Makan Gobi and the deserts of Central Asia. Scholars therefore dubbed that road the "Desert Silk Road" to differentiate it from the "Grass Silk Road" to its north and the "Silk Road on the Sea" over the seas in the Southwest.

The Silk Road like a brilliant ribbon linked up the Orient with the West for a dozen centuries. This East-West trading passage served as a vital lever for the Chinese civilization on the world history as well as a window for China to know and assimilate other civilizations of the world.

Jiaohe ancient city, a famous city along the Silk Road, has a history of more than 2,000 years. It is the most well-preserved and the largest city built with soil in the world.

The Hall of Supreme Harmony, the highest-grade hall in the Forbidden City

When you are having a bird's eye view of Beijing on top of the Jingshan Hill at the back of the Forbidden City, you marvel at the glitteringly yellow roofs of the Imperial Palace. And inside the palaces, you will be impressed by the golden ceilings, the gilded throne and the giant gilded pillars and the exquisitely gold-thread embroidered yellow "dragon robes" of the former emperors. The color of yellow, you find, used to be the monopoly of the feudal emperors who wielded the supreme monarchal power.

The imperial palaces of the Ming and Qing dynasties were all built with yellow-glazed tiles. All color-glazed tiles were luxury building materials in old China, but only those of yellow color were used in the imperial palaces, tomb and temples. The use of yellow-glazed tiles on some special buildings, such as the Temple of Confucius, won the personal approval of the emperor. That is why all the dwellings of the ordinary people outside the Imperial Palace were covered with gray tiles and bricks, with no exception for the courtyard compounds.

The inside of the splendid looking Hall of Supreme Harmony

Emperor Qianlong of the Qing Dynasty in his official robe

Chun Hui Imperial Concubine of the Qing Dynasty in her official robe

In the Chinese history, there was a story about the yellow robe. The story says that in 959, one emperor died and his young son succeeded to the throne. The following year, General Zhao Kuangyin who controlled the army was draped a yellow robe over his shoulders by his subordinates and supported him to be the new emperor. Why did the "yellow robe" represent the emperor?

At an earlier time, the Chinese emperors did not wear yellow garments. For example, black was in fashion and the emperor and officials all wore black garments in the Qin Dynasty.

Emperor Wudi (reigned 140–87 BC) of the Western Han Dynasty was the first emperor who favored the color of yellow. Since then, yellow gradually became the highest grade color for garments. However, ordinary people were not banned to wear yellow clothes. After the Tang Dynasty, a decree was issued that aside from the emperor, officials and ordinary people were not allowed to wear yellow garment. This decree was effective until China's last feudal society — the Qing Dynasty.

COLORFUL CHINA

Try to ask people where the most brilliant yellow color on earth comes from and the most likely answer would be GOLD!

Small wonder, love and worship for gold can be said to be a global inclination. There were very bright gold cultures in ancient Egypt, Greece and the Two-River Valley. Relatively, ancient Chinese did not show such fervor for gold but Chinese gold culture had its own features.

The earliest gold ornaments discovered in China were unearthed from tombs of the Xia Dynasty dating back to more than four thousand years ago. Despite the long history of the use of gold in China, the Chinese people however focused their love primarily on bronze articles for more than a millennium from the third century B.C. on. In that period, gold was used generally for secondary decoration in the manufacturing of bronze articles.

The technology of gold inlaying grew mature and a gold handicraft skill independent from that of bronze making was believed to take place roughly in the third century before Christ. The opening of the Silk Road brought in gold articles from the West which inspired Chinese handicraft masters to assimilate the alien cultural elements in the manufacturing of gold articles. The handicraft art of gold articles advanced progressively and became increasingly sophisticated with the designing, coloring and decorations.

Over the past centuries, gold was eulogized and cursed at the same time by people. However, the gold articles as objects of art made by past masters have attained a lasting glamour. They are not merely embodiment of wealth, but precious footprints of history and civilization.

The golden food containers of the Warring States period (475–256 BC)

The golden pagoda of the Qing Dynasty

COLORFUL CHINA

There is a saying in China that it is easy to get gold but it is hard to gain *Tianhuang* stone. The *Tianhuang* stone, believed to be more precious than gold, is in fact a special stone with the main color of yellow.

The *Tianhuang* stone is precious because it is rare. Its place of origin is a piece of field of about one square kilometer at Shoushan, Fujian Province. Its formation originates from the geological changes between 230 million and 67 million years ago: the lava erupted from the volcano melted with the surrounding rocks and crystallized after cooling down to become the ore. After that, the ore was flown into the creek. After washing by the water and nourishing by the earth, it formed the wonderful color, mild texture and delicate patterns.

People love to use *Tianhuang* stone to make seals. At the Palace Museum, there is a collection of such seals used by Emperor Qianlong, Empress Dowager Cixi (1835–1908). The craftsmen make full use of the natural color, shape and patterns to carve various figures, mountains and water, flowers and birds. The works are delicate and enjoyed by both highbrows and lowbrows.

Baopu Taoist Temple in Hangzhou, Zhejiang Province

Taoism is a religion originated from China. It has a history of more than 1,800 years. In the early times, Taoist priest wore yellow garments and hats. Therefore, it has its nickname of "Yellow Hat". Later, Taoist priest changed to wear blue robes. However, while being initiated into monkhood or nunhood, or in services, the priest will wear yellow robes.

COLORFUL CHINA

Monks at Baima Temple, Luoyang, Henan Province

The Chinese Buddhism was originated from ancient India. It entered China at the middle of the first century. It has produced significant impact to the ancient society and culture of China. The Buddhism believes that yellow (including goldenness) symbolizes being free from vulgarities. It is the magnificence of Buddhist doctrine. Therefore, its constructions, garments and containers are all in yellow: The Buddhist temple is called "golden temple"; the Buddhist is called "golden body"; the statues of Buddha are mostly gilded or made of pure gold; the monks wear yellow garments; the offering and ritual implement are mostly gilded with gold; some people even copy Buddhist scripts with gold…

The gold gilded statue of Buddha at Jokhang Monastery in Lhasa ▶

Chapter on
Red

Of all colors, red is most lively and buoyant. Red, the color of fire and the sun, is the color of vigor and excitement.

Red is the symbol of China and red is the prettiest color in the minds of the Chinese people. Ever since the ancient time, the lives of the Chinese people have been filled with all sorts of red themes, ranging from the red decorations on all occasions of celebrations, the large red lanterns conveying a sense of peace and happiness, red walls signifying power and dignity, to the expression of people's emotions and thinking in the color of red. Perhaps only the Chinese in this world are capable of giving a myriad implications to the color of red at great liberty.

The Chinese red has been a heavy sedimentation of the 5000-year old Chinese culture. It has been deeply rooted in the Chinese soul. It has been the color totem to the Chinese generation after generation.

In Southern China, there are vast areas that have red earth grown under the warm and rainy conditions.

The red land in Dongchuan, Yunnan Province, is believed to be the most grand red earth in the world aside from Rio de Janeiro of Brazil. In Dongchuan, layers of red earth ladder field can be seen in a area with a diameter of several hundred kilometers. Because local people usually rotate planting on some parts of the red earth while idling the other parts, the green agriculture field looks like inlaid in the red field. Adding to the different flowers of various plants in blossom in turns in different seasons, the land is decorated with different colors of red, green, white and yellow. The mixture of the color makes of a strong color pad and as if it is paved to the end of the land.

COLORFUL CHINA

Danxia geomorphology refers the solitary peak and cliff rocks formed after the red gravel rocks have long been weathered away and eroded. Currently, there are altogether 1,200 such geomorphology in the world. Among them, more than 700 are in China.

The Chinese feudal emperors in the past showed a particular love for red. The former Imperial Palace in Beijing which consists of nearly a thousand rooms covering a total building area of 720,000 square meters are in red and yellow. The red-painted gates and the yellow-glazed tiles give the Forbidden City a majestic view when looked at a distance. Inside the pavilions, all the pillars are painted red to show the imperial power and solemnity. Red was also the color in which Chinese emperors wrote mandates on reports from officials, for red was considered a color of authority.

COLORFUL CHINA

R ed is the special color when Chinese stamp a seal.
Since ancient times, seal has been an important tool to indicate the identity and power in China. The seal of ancient emperor was called "royal seal", symbolizing the imperial power; seals used by officials and administrations at various levels were called public seals and issued by the emperor; ordinary people used seals that have their names carved; scholars used their own seals to mark on calligraphies and paintings. Therefore, the content of the seal has a great variety and becomes interesting; for unlettered people, they had their own special seal — their fingerprint. Till now, seal is still the most important proof of official documents and plays an important role in people's life.

In the eyes of Chinese people, seal is something to show good faith. It shows earnest commitment and strict credit and is the proof of exchanges and mutual trust. The eye-catching yet solemn color of red is exactly the color that conveys the credit of a seal.

"Chinese Seal — Dancing Beijing", the emblem of the Beijing Olympic Games in 2008

The rosewood (or mahogany) furniture with dark red color is favored by Chinese due to its elegance and luxury.

The period between 15th century and 17th century, or about the mid-Ming Dynasty and early Qing Dynasty, was the prime time for traditional Chinese rosewood furniture. The mahogany furniture produced at the time was the essence of the classic furniture of China. The furniture usually selects quality hard wood of red sandalwood, yellow pear wood, old iron wood. The colors are steady and quietly elegant; Its shape is simple with swift lines; all the joints of the furniture rely on tenon and mortise without any nails.

COLORFUL CHINA

The red mask in Peking Opera generally portrays a faithful and upright character. For example, General Guan Yu of the Three Kingdom period (220–280) was a sworn brother of Liu Bei. The two later turned to form a king-and-official relation. Under whatever situations, Guan Yu was faithful to him and supported him. In the eyes of ordinary people, Guan Yu is a symbol of loyalty. People honored him as "Guan Gong" or "God of War". There are many Guandi temples where Guan Yu was worshipped.

In the first lunar month, Miao nationality people, young and old, at Kaili, Guizhou Province will paint their faces red and carry gifts to visit neighboring stockades and relatives. According to local customs of the Miao nationality, they should paint their faces red on important occasions or festivals or having distinguished guests.

COLORFUL CHINA

Every household is busy hanging lanterns, sticking on Festival couplets and New Year pictures to greet the New Year.

Spring Lantern fair at Lantern Festival

The Spring Festival which marks the beginning of the Lunar New Year is a Chinese folk holiday. Of all Chinese traditional holidays, the Chinese attach the greatest importance to Spring Festival, throughout which festivity reaches a new climax with verve, warmth, greetings and best wishes, all wrapped in the color of red.

One meaningful custom related Spring Festival is the pasting on doors red-paper spring couplet scrolls. The content of the couplets usually conveys good wishes for the New Year. In addition to the red-paper couplet scrolls, people also like to have square red-paper posters written with a large character "福" meaning "happy lot" pasted on the main entrance to their houses. Red lanterns are hung from the eaves and red paper cuts are pasted on window glasses, meaning the arrival of good luck. In the countryside, farmers like to past pictures of "Door Gods" on their doors to ward off evils. Inside, they like to paste New Year pictures with happy contents on the walls. All of the pictures are also printed on red paper.

In the first month of the Lunar New Year, people like to put on new clothes and exchange visits and greetings with relatives and friends. Children are very happy to get *yasuiqian* (cash gifts) in red envelopes from their seniors as a gesture of well wishing. Also wrapped in red paper are firecrackers which children like to let off during the festival.

Despite the fact that people in modern Chinese cities today find the strong festivity of Spring Festival is waning, the color of red still stands out in the streets of Chinese cities during the festival. In short, Spring Festival is celebrated in red color as the keynote permeates throughout the country as a perpetual traditional flavor unique to Spring Festival.

Entertainment activity in the Spring Festival: Lion Dancing ▶

COLORFUL CHINA

The red wedding ceremony attracts many foreign friends.

The color of bright red more than any other colors is apt to convey the lively and joyous atmosphere at a traditional Chinese wedding and red has become the symbolic color of Chinese weddings just like pure white of bridal gowns at Western weddings.

On the day of wedding, early in the morning, the groom dressed in red gown adorned with a big red flower on his chest, then escorted by the go-between and wedding attendants, the bridegroom followed the red bridal sedan to pick up the bride at the bride's home. The bride was dressed in embroidered red dress and skirt and wore a red silk veil. After the bride bade farewell by kowtowing to her parents, the procession left for the bridegroom's home. On arrival, the bride entered the main hall of the groom's home which was gaily decorated with a large red paper-cut of the character of "囍" which means "double happiness" and red silk streamers and festoon. The wedding formally began with the couple kowtowing first to the Heaven and the Earth, then to the groom's parents and finally to each other. After the ceremony concluded, the bride and bridegroom were escorted into their nuptial bedroom which was decorated practically in a sea of red articles including red candles, red double happiness posters, red curtains and red bed spread…

On modern Chinese weddings, in addition to red posters of double happiness and red dresses, more red elements are added, such as red invitation cards, candies with red wrapping, red festoons adorning the bridal sedans, bouquets of red peonies, etc. Meanwhile more and more people like the romantic touch of white bridal dresses, but the love for the red color stays and many Chinese modern weddings are a mixture of the Chinese style and the Western style.

The wedding photo of a rural couple

Among the people in China, red is considered as a kind of color that can help people avoid inauspiciousness and disaster.

Whenever a baby is born to a family, people will present boiled egged dyed into red to relatives, friends and neighbors on the first day of the birth or on the one-month anniversary. The color of red represents happiness. To give out red eggs is to share the happiness with others. At the same time, red also represents life, indicating that the parents of the family hope the child can lead a peaceful and happy life. In many places, the new-born baby needs to wear a red apron and red tiger-head shoes. People believe that red can help drive away evils and bless a healthy growth to the baby.

Whenever it comes the year of the animal in which one was born, people will wear red underwear and tie red belt. The recurrent year in the 12-year cycle of the same animal is unique in China. Beginning from the year one was born, he or she will meet the year of animal in which he or she was born every 12 years. Because the year is usually considered as unlucky, people need to use red to keep away the wickedness.

These ancient customs have been passed down till today. Although people do not believe that red will help drive away disasters now, they are willing to accept the auspiciousness of this traditional way.

Rural child wearing a red apron

◀ The red tiger-head shoes

COLORFUL CHINA

The waist-drum team at the Loess Plateau

The red chili is also regarded as a symbol of prosperity.

Folk paper-cutting usually uses red as a symbol of auspiciousness and happiness.

COLORFUL CHINA

The Potala Palace in Lhasa

Lamas discuss Buddhist scripts.

From the burning sunshine to people's face, from rows of monastery to the kasaya of the Lamas, red can be seen everywhere in Tibet.

Red and white is the most common colors in the Tibetan architecture. White symbolizes peace and good deeds while red the strength and power. The grand Potala Palace is the site where every Dalai Lama live and conduct political and religious activities. Its buildings are divided into the Red Palace and the White Palace. The Red Palace is situated in the center and top of the Potala. The memorial pagodas of previous Dalai Lamas are kept there.

COLORFUL CHINA

The development of the Chinese language is also indicative of the Chinese people's love for red over the centuries. For example, people refer the young ladies as "red complexions," good luck as "red luck," and a superior's favorite as "so and so's 'red person'."

The Red Yao living in Longsheng, Guangxi is a branch of the Yao nationality. Because their clothes are mainly red, they are called "Red Yao".

At the "Miss World" held in Sanya, Hainan Province, the young girls wear Chinese *qipao*, the close-fitting woman's dress with high neck and slit skirt. In people's minds, only the red color is capable of best conveying the Chinese grace and elegance.

The T-stage of the fashion world is getting increasingly red. Since mid-1990s, this color of the Orient has been gaining ground in the fashion world across the globe. Furthermore, Chinese Red is spreading to world famous porcelain ware, jewelry, home decoration articles, cloth, etc.

COLORFUL CHINA

The red Chinese palace walls, red lanterns, red weddings, red New Year door scrolls, and many other things in red all bear the red theme in the lives of the Chinese people for thousands of years. Red is a color of good omens, a color for celebration. Red is the hallmark color of Chinese customs and habits and Chinese culture. Red is symbolic of China in the minds of the Chinese people. Bright red recognized as Chinese Red has become a particular member of the family of colors.

The Chinese Red is classic and modern, reserved and buoyant at the same time. The color seems mute, but it is speaking loudly about China, about the Chinese people and the Chinese culture.

Chinese fans cheer for the Chinese football team.

On the night of January 24, 2004, the Eiffel Tower instantly turned red when 240 red lights on the banks of the Seine River were switched on. The Tower changed into a red garment to mark the Chinese Spring Festival and particularly the 40th anniversary of the establishment of diplomatic relations between China and France. ▶

图书在版编目（CIP）数据

多彩中国：英文/梁敏玲著；刘炳文,潘忠明译. —北京：五洲传播出版社,
2007.8（2008.5重印）
ISBN 978-7-5085-1080-4

Ⅰ.多... Ⅱ.①梁...②刘...③潘... Ⅲ.传统文化—中国—英文 Ⅳ.G12

中国版本图书馆CIP数据核字（2007）第064552号

多彩中国

撰　　　文：梁敏玲
翻　　　译：刘炳文　潘忠明
图片提供：张超音　全景视觉　东方IC　China Foto Press
责任编辑：苏　谦
装帧设计：闫志杰
篇章页书法题字：常健君
设计制作：刘　娜　真　真

出版发行：五洲传播出版社
地　　　址：北京市海淀区北小马厂6号
邮　　　编：100038
网　　　址：http://www.cicc.org.cn
电　　　话：010-58891281
印　　　刷：北京华联印刷有限公司
字　　　数：25千字
图　　　片：140幅
开　　　本：787×1092mm　1/16
印　　　张：9.5
印　　　数：5001-15000册
版　　　次：2007年8月第1版　2008年5月第2次印刷
定　　　价：98.00元